SLEEPING WITH PLATO

ELIZA STEFANIDI

SLEEPING WITH PLATO

LYRICAL FRAGMENTS
FOR THE DIGITAL AGE

 EYEWEAR PUBLISHING

First published in 2015
by Eyewear Publishing Ltd
74 Leith Mansions, Grantully Road
London W9 1LJ
United Kingdom

Illustrations and art by Eliza Stefanidi
Cover design and typeset by Edwin Smet
Author photograph by Thomas Poravas
Printed in England by TJ International Ltd, Padstow, Cornwall

All rights reserved
© 2015 Eliza Stefanidi

The right of Eliza Stefanidi to be identified as author of this work has been asserted in accordance with section 77 of the Copyright, Designs and Patents Act 1988
ISBN 978-1-908998-83-5

Eyewear wishes to thank Jonathan Wonham *for his very generous patronage of our press; as well as our other patrons and investors who wish to remain anonymous.*

WWW.EYEWEARPUBLISHING.COM

To my parents, Diomedes and Eurydice.
Sisters, Maria and Pascalle.
To my twin nephews, Diomedes and Jason.

We will still have each other. Even if some people, but most of all we and I too, feel sometimes Earth's ground and light's touch are not around.

A citizen of both Britain and Greece, Eliza Stefanidi was born in Liverpool in 1980. She has an intermediate diploma in ballet from the Royal Academy of Dance and a BA in Media and Culture Studies from The London College of Printing. Diagnosed with bipolar disorder at the age of 24 she has made issues of mental, linguistic, and social crisis her main themes in her art and writing. She currently lives in Athens.

Table of Contents

The Chase — 11
Cosmic Jeanne D'Arc — 12
Like it (or not) — 13
Mind a mind trap — 14
One memory track — 15
Hell O mom — 16
Suspense Strategy — 17
Lucid Laces — 18
Progressive Happiness — 19
Liverpool Grounds — 20
A dialogue for the lady — 21
Motel Mona Lisa — 22
Traditional Formula — 24
Poetic Complex — 25
Valentine's Day — 26
Take it easy on me — 27
Company — 28
Boys & Girls — 29
Fair comments are welcomed — 30
Paused and Eager — 31
To — 32
Graceful Restart — 33
Process Love — 34
For the first time — 35
Reminder — 36
Rupturing — 37
Dear — 38
The point of the bridge — 40
You and I — 41
Building Up — 42
Yes (revisited) — 43
Cali Brake — 44

Lowest of lows — 45
Fields — 46
Nobody Understood — 47
Days go by and bend — 48
Sleeping With Plato — 49
Forever — 50
Romantics — 51
Lazy and niche — 52
Cantina Social — 53
This red floor — 54
Marilyn's Instagram photo — 55
Guinness & Bacardi — 56
Joyrides — 57
Asclepius and Hippocrates — 58
Nearly Subconscious — 59
We — 61
Eccentric Witches — 62
Full-length Youth — 63
He — 64
In Doubt — 65
Miss Nice — 66
Balcony Translations — 67
Numbers — 68
Clouds — 69
Silver Crown When You Come Around — 70
Full Moon — 71
24 Hours — 72
Paper Panic — 73
London to Utopia — 74
When you lose — 76

Acknowledgements — 79

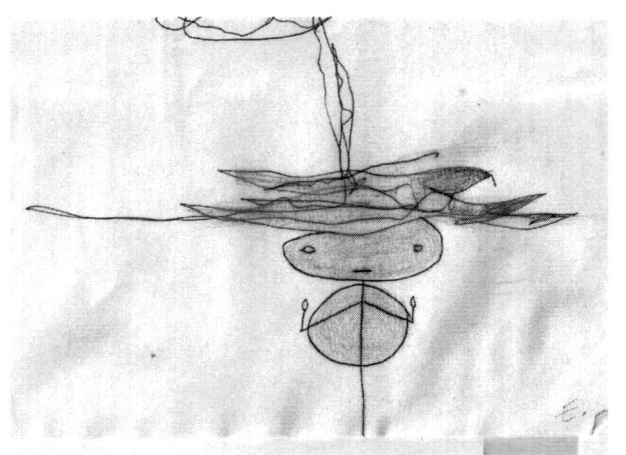

Youth knows no pain
　　— Lykke Li

A crack of light falls around me
　　— Denise Riley

You must think that something is happening with you…
　　— Rainer Maria Rilke

The Chase

Possess your frequencies
Post your requirements
Pin up your mind advice
Lung courage fails
Night calling out names
Bipolar tendencies sounds fearful
It's hard to explain the chase

Cosmic Jeanne D'Arc

Nikon pictures of my subconscious struck my blindness last night.
My little Sophia, Maria Christina, I think you are almost there,
with your Beaufort, bouncy, ballerina steps.

You and your high and low opera voices
always touch ground to never brake
to seek for one single emotional mode.

To breathe under thousands of Chopin and Liszt notes.
And all gods yes are stuck there between
a beloved Steinway and following Sons.

And still friends of friends haunt my nights.
To find out why and how some old souls
pretend to always pretend to stay young.

And still you, my friends of friends, wonder how
a cosmic Jeanne D'Arc heard voices, got burnt
and sang no hallelujah songs. Well please don't be scared

of His Good Friday's actual strong voice.
It sounds like Easter Sunday's morning glory and fireworks,
drained by all the might of birds flying above our heads.

Like it (or not)

Did you like it; would you lock it,
there under a first name?
Under 'Love', Αγάπη',
under a brand name
of strippers, professional sinners
and trippers. Did you like it;
would you stop it,
there upon your college facts and figures?
Upon one memory collage, bricolage,
upon the same name of unwise mind
frames, of the same sabotage games?
Did you like it; or not
there where this world refuses to sink well
there where 'Taylor' and 'Niki'
have a little cat spat?
Would you police us to see,
police me; to find my way home,
police us; for a change?
For a chain gang and 'chin to chin',
lost plane people picture drain?
Would you like it; or not?
Would you; for us to find
some homegrown happy pigeons,
religions? Did you or not?
We need to find one lucky
smoky stone and a sacred same love.

Mind a mind trap

mind a mind trap; mind gap
mind all fast lanes and mind games

mind a piece of mind and repeat
mind all brain cells; proceed

One memory track

On a blue urban roof top
Topped and iced with poetry
Ways. It's OK. A-Okays

Don't play with one memory track
Two, three overplayed & overused hearts
Some day *they* might all, all come back

Hell O mom

Hell O mom.
Dial zero; to reach my numb diagonal smile and frown
Dial one; to pray for my darkness and my hyperactive unborn son
You see, if you dial me, delete me, scratch me, with soft sounds
I might sing louder than your tears and colours.
And stand like a statue, that never walked straight.
And be silent all the way through your eyes.
Hell O mom.
Don't worry when I bow and dance all around.
When we both bow to all mothers' pride, with some prophets
and tender seraphs and Angels.
Angel: what a common small word.
See, you can dial me to reach a place to walk free.
Free as hell; oh mom. My heart; dial zero,
to preach a psychotic, chaotic breath, to feed my head.
Dial one; as I board beaches around trees and shape strange tongues.
Mom; dial two for a change; for I'm not anymore in pain,
when they call my name. For I learned by now
to hide well a bilingual Ace of spade (s). Up my mind's sleeve.
I'll say now; Sail now, a nice hello
and smile like your supportive silence. Hello mom.
I might answer your turbulent urge with one unborn son.
O, Hell O; son.

Suspense Strategy

So it began, a supportive one way strategy.
This town seems to have errors in all corners.

Lucid Laces

White uniforms unite behind; trammeled doors
Swore mercy; denies your humanity
Jesus let me try; give me your timeworn wood
Lend me your shoes; and I'll tie your lucid laces

Progressive Happiness

Whistling to a bad day; shouting for a better one.
Predicting progressive happiness out of this semi-pastel box.
I and all them I's, inform a 'full-length youth' to centralise.
Fifty per cent data collected from within; giving these eyes
way too much chance to mystify again. Your sun's in sync;
Mr. Postman it's two forty five a.m.; passing a mindless mission.
Envelope says: 'no ethical parameters on your side, no parameters'.
No sins, 'you have no sins'. For yesterday was blue, tomorrow is low;
too slow, begging for a lonesome harm might shut your shutters down.
Will you predict progressive happiness out of a semi-pastel box?
And now you are whistling again; for it's a good day, and all smiles
love all 'get well' calls and all, all, lost and found, familiar words.

Liverpool grounds

These sounds are echoing
some past London based confusions.
These Liverpool grounds promised my visual birth
and denied my death a long time ago.
Speaking to a brave page, I wonder;
what will happen, if you were to be bleached
with anesthesia and purified with intentions.
Super girls behave and fall apart.
Sometimes I wish
I was hyperlinked to become a steep metaphor of myself.
This young night, I gather information
around heavy-placed ideas.
Stepped backwards and took a look down English streets.
Sympathy said, 'stop razing your pens'.
Amplified ballet walks begged for more.

A dialogue for the lady

Blonde make up, red lipstick, few drinks.
Lady walks down the street.
She goes in simple verse.
Claims her name belongs to a famous Christmas carol.
'It's only December. Remember?'
'It's only December. Remember?'
repeating herself she looks petite
this sunny morning near
the local chapel.
'If I fall. If. I'll cry ',
'If I fall. If. I'll die';
misleading us, the near neighbors
just watch and just hear.
And as she starts pulsing
an English song out of her hood
and almost out of her mouth,
this guy screams like a funny killer from a balcony:
'This is not America.'
'If you fall. Please don't sing',
'If you fall. Die lady. Please.'
This blonde make up. This bloody lipstick just had
a few morning drinks.
Lady crawls down our street.
She goes in simple verse.
Simply calls for a simple cause.
Denies her name belongs to a famous Christmas carol.
 'Y'all wanna drink. My Lord. Good God.'

Motel Mona Lisa

Bless and fill this room with sudden, flamboyant thunder;
as hunger swings with no laughter.
As we pretend to pay; are we all here to find
a wise way, one way. As an unforgettable vanity
and humble thirst, that sings slow, through your brain tonight.
Because that's the way, I steal
rhymes and verses; no, please don't search for looks,
down and underneath
book lines and all gone faces.

Try not to hate heaven sent crooks, gods speed
and races. Do you still marvel as far as we can dream,
linger all breathless.
Because, that's the way we do the things
we do and scare our family members.
When our dosed half
becomes a silent mood singer and drowns against blurry faces;
pretend to pay one way. Oh, this could be a real hide and seek,
fun sick game. The way
we live, change or just another curious way.
Well as for me, *I fought you and we won*;
found you and my frown is all gone.
As you go higher and higher and trust me; one September's
day light, line and free figure, free. As our roads meet,
searching notions, e-cautions, electric
motions, inside true shadow plays and blossoms and giggles.
Someone please, shake
our real dreams that shutter our world, and pray.
Motel Mona Lisa is my face, a real name reflected
on a real mirror; hey there, hey.
Your fortune face, stares your heartbox. You're a real
face this time that lights up my race. Bless the water
and fill this room with cold thunder; rule our
heartbeat, a one hit wonder. Wake up and free some twin souls
and find ourselves locked up in a good yes or no.
Because that's the way I live and stay;
hear a loud morning and dawning and say, pray.
No distance between you and beside my emotion.

Traditional Formula

Urging an improvement like a child;
on a traditional sky formula without strict strings attached
complete movements go in circle and circles.
An agony gently removed;
mostly like these red contact lenses you've been wearing
to gaze on your image of spin.
When all my unplugged friends explain feelings and voices
this Music is not loud. This oak band performs a perfect sound;
honestly kneeling to wooden guitars and their roll history.

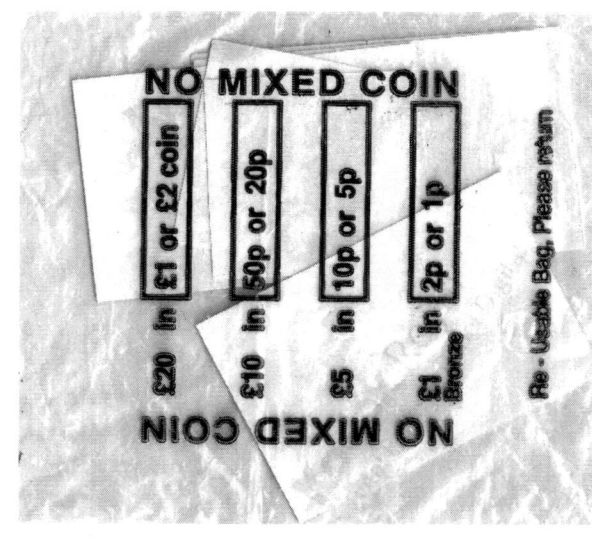

Poetic Complex

Your complexity strangles my throat
and breaks my neck
Dear your complexity wears me out
from now; from then

from steep nights; from anything
from everything
Dear your complexity rests
and lies down uncomfortably;

safely to a hundred couches
of faraway obstacles; that is why
that is why today your steps
are not identified; that is why today

a poetic complex finds a place to hide
What a day to hide underneath; to last a decade
As nights go red and weeks go by
time underneath time that takes too much time

Valentine's Day

All I care for is music
All you care for is music
All we care about
Are rescue boats

The ones that rock your guts
That stop your heart, you know
From zero, to minus zero
All we care for is stupid love, true love

No love at all sir, madam, kids
Figure two, figure four, figure eight
Figure it out, love
All you care for is stand-up

All we are is comedy
Boats sink; guts wrench; needles skip
Hearts scratch and zero falls down to zero
Where no music plays, no shouts

Take it easy on me

O mother, father, sisters, blisters,
Let us all pray for you, for the USA,
For Ukraine, for me. For a lost plane.
For sinners, winners, sad Vodka songs.
All prayers are twisters; to those
Who save lives; who save pride at sea.
I want to belong to this. Go easy
Although I won't make it easy for us.
Hold me as your new child if you can.
I know you can't keep love alive
Once the radar's been clicked
So beacons sends ships off-course.
There is no because, only harms
From humans, with their casual arms.

Company

Might you say it will last all day
might you always say it will drift for the night
like terrible honesty would
like a buzz in my ear I've heard before
like a quiet company making noise
like past breaks a future
might you say 'anything would'

Boys & Girls

Tiny me, in need of a 'Think big' idea.
His 'Busy bee's' silence is slipping through a hole in my pocket
like a thick colourful mess.
This is not about crawling, begging, falling
or even about a cheerful blessed Good morning.

Fair comments are welcomed

Through this fair comment of a slow salty night
After the dark nests of your 'I'm so happy' religion
Sleeping next to my mute and clock wise friends
Plus one, plus three.
All together in a sticker smart packed van
Pretty eyes heading south, she said *I'll be fine by then*,
Be fine by them.
Concentrated dear friends, try to
Comprehend the simplicity of your lakeside walks
Around *this thing we call life*.
There is an animal institution
That burns, instantly, our tiny deserted light.

Paused and Eager

Steep confrontations.
Walking back to basics; nothing is denial.
Now and then; then and *A pause*.
Pause and the breaks.
Why-misinterpretations.
Waking up to rules; spoken to anything.
Now and then. Then and *A pause*.
Paused and *Eager* seem too familiar
Something's *Never* begins to fail.

To

to mercy
to madness
to wealth and poverty
to them that sunk
to all of us we call people and tangle stories with Medea
is your sanity perfect
is your dignity crystal clear

Graceful Restart

fabricated ordinate surprises
somebody is heavenly wasting time
subscribe frustrations safely to your pillow
and spare me the beauty of your plans
enter, shift these beliefs
threefold information of doubts
what it takes to move around a poetic rhythm
such a tangle of effortless artful games
too close. these case studies of bracelet epilogues
and currencies of a word called empathy
i follow my bent
and board beaches around trees
still, i filter your taste and let sea gulls reveal,
bounded, grounded to a graceful restart

Process Love

Compatible with nature's law
Anything escapes everything
Processed in a shadow box
Love, the ultimate
Instant for what is worth it
Plausible if it rocks and rolls

For the first time

Crashed cars shook a near handled loss
like a pretty good yes made in most black and white films
unwinding the dear calling of a pleased to become;
so high and so patient for the first time

This is an immense paralysed moment
this is me smiling back at our ships and relations
Good wills; all spoken in shock
Tricks and Treats; stood right there in front

Untying my deep confessions as someone special was observing
wisely my back; for the first time
Oh boys we can drink to this versus our knowledge
of how and why; of let's not die

Pretty damn good riddance and a survival
causing headaches to some still wannabe stillness
There was this silence; this animated alarm
causing harmless words to pass out; for the first time.

Reminder

Remind me when I forget, forget to mention you
Remind me folks; remind me, believe me
You taste like forgotten days
Remind me folks; remind me red London blocks
Harmless faces; unwind people, surprise me
Break water, plants, sweet berries and sand
Like a faded hand washed yellow and black;
Remind me when I forget, forget to mention you
Your sick nests, homegrown religion breaths
Forgot all about mysterious mind
Murderous and adjustable;
Numb circles and high healthy corners abound.
Nothing is real, real is Something.

Rupturing

Musical boxes of my rhythms;
Athenian nights, universal spectators
Your eager skinny soul graved my empathy;
Cheer leaders, toxic breeders; will wait till tomorrow
And raping history's monologue is right under our colour print feet.

Rupturing guerrilla nightmares, screaming frustrating forgiveness;
could we touch faith's grimness

Well, his threesome quests never entered my neuron Trans meters;
he might appoint the f word difference

Dear

Dear they say all it takes is one second;
darling that's all it takes to 'fold' pain.
My love a peach bed was stolen last night;
thank God we both need another type of night.

Dear now we all hate Mondays;
darling let's pretend we ate those sun days.
My love scratches are supposed to last less;
thank God he provides for us, the best.

Dear seems like we are completely broken;
darling you know the truth lies down to nothing.
My love watch now, we are walking;
thank God we are still walking.

Dear let's obsess over the chase;
darling sometimes I know it's hard to explain to the rest.
My love we used to think letters made words;
thank God sounds are still found in songs.

Dear we could live and share;
darling we might someday sing to dare.
My love those demons are surely hiding;
thank God they are still hiding.

Dear we used to wake up to no rules;
darling now sleep with no fools.
My love angels sometimes dress up in black t shirts;
thank God some still wear those black t-shirts.

Dear never think of how to fix strings;
darling please think of how to think.
My love take care of those blue kids;
thank God, God took care of his things.

The point of the bridge

'Life is slow under a free top shot'

O romance is chemically stolen
And I guess it was always about a bridge
When he said he might buy the bridge
Of my troubled waters, he made me smile

And I guess some of us wait forever
Phone won't ring so we'll eat your numbers
Change these darling minds, worry not
Change there, under our numb names

Don't fail; there's always someone shouting wait
Tripping as we feel.
Stay away from a Plastic Dreamland
Alone and so tonight.

This Monday is like
He's turning his back to one hundred miles
When some loving spells and dogs
Knock on back doors

We welcome instant promises.
We all welcome remote sweet somethings
We hold mobile phones; we have mobile hearts
We still ought; we still owe.

You and I

'If you're going through hell, keep going' – Winston Churchill

Run my darling; run all this you speed and hurry
Drink my darling; drink all this you round and bury

Crush my darling; crush all this you hide and get
Fix my darling; fix all this you shoot and mend

Eat my darling; eat all this you catch and find
Spend my darling; spend all this you kick and mind

Promise my darling; promise all this you miss and hit
Want my darling; want all this you kiss and stitch

Trust my darling; trust all this you speak and touch
Run my darling; run all this you claim and clutch

Break my darling; break all this you mean and glue
'Hey' my darling; 'hey' all those you goodbye and sue

You my darling; you are all I need, to not flip and drop
Stay my darling; stay. That's all I'll say and stop.

Building Up

Want this bad news feed back
Want these good news hot breaks
Want one silent rain drop
Want two neon signs of 'yes'
Want alive posts and re-posts
Want dead stones and rolling 'wills'
Want to build up memories
Want to be solitary and wrong
Want something to play it cool
Want one day to play the fool
Want to talk with no creep; enough echo, repeat

Yes (revisited)

No priorities
No apologies
No dreams
No screams
No existence
No sisters
No twisters
No thoughts
No clocks
No maybe
No baby
No something
No nothing
No candles
No suns
No bandages
No stitches
No phones
No clones
No darlings
No strings
No blinks
No shrinks
No drinks
No yes
No tables
Turned no
To yes

Yes

No dear
No Sir
No mothers
No fathers
No friends
No frustrations
No sense
No bees
No trees
No offence
No applications
No doubt
No account
Not about
No drinking
No buses
No degradations
No sickness
No health
No answers
Not great
No Hate

I's,
Not all of them,
them I's are equal
Locked up in a Yes
You
Look so distressed
holding your keys

Cali Brake

Meet California
on your way back home
as she undresses her neighbours
gives them the sun
all the magnificence
pedal brakes
and all you care about
is sunshine driving
back pack unwinding
dosed to become
one of your favorites,
dosed and getting away
with California

Lowest of lows

A pen
sharpens any thought; any 'might'
A whore
wallows in any hand; on every 'man'
One
breaks bones to find flesh; an uninfected chest
One
tears pages to find meaning; bricks, silver linings, 'healing'
Someone
is pausing the limits of the psyche; of any single mind and mind
No one
can pause the limits of one; of two, of singles and twins,
of all that touch the lowest of lows and all the rest that
        follows and flows
Just because
two of you felt it
Just because
all of us break
and amend it

Fields

Of summer hints
Of one strained present and two futures
Of fast turns brought from fun, harm, fun
Of instant currencies bought from a man
And I can't fall asleep
Emotions flip under a colour field
Of many versions of you
Loving each stereo star;
Meaning every blink so far

Nobody Understood

As we were standing on the edge of awaking
Two men noticed the difference between us
Stood there mute
Just like they were playing the game
You know gaining points
In pitch black final positions
Looking for common sense

Days go by and bend

Hungry fourteen. Girls' basketball diaries.
Waking up. Doing some thinking.

Making plans. Now you do.
As we take our *go slow* ways. Longing for friendships.

Now you are figuring it out.
Having a voice. Now you don't.

Send the bending over here.
As the last man on earth steals words from worlds.

This is what you get with books, music, drama and pills.
This is what you get as days go by and bend.

A drive through the *might* and *because*.
A Soundtrack. Emotional stuff and magazines.

Weak.
Weeks again.

When we first take home our religion.
Sometimes absence needs absence.

Sleeping With Plato

and I sleep with strange silence by my side
and I sleep with weird words under my pillow
oh Plato where are you hiding tonight?

(when) a beat turns your head around
(when) a beat turns your head upside down
before you go to bed so early

before you run away from me
before you think too wisely
before you pray for me and rise

if it's all about love will you stretch your arm for me?
can you show me a dialogue?
can you show me lies?

look I'm standing so innocently
look I'm standing in no sense my dear

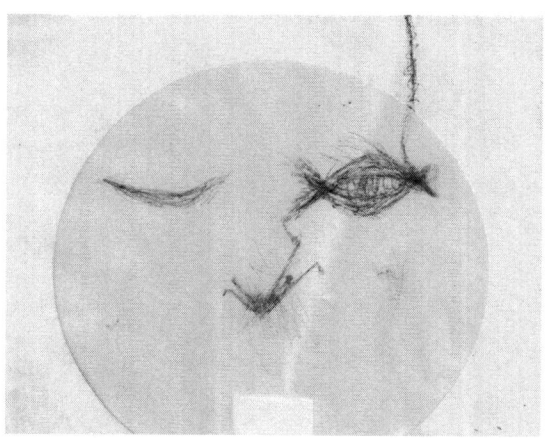

Forever

Never said; red ribbons won't bleach.
Never said; can read minds. Offer mute minutes.
Never said; yellow ribbons won't untangle voices.
Never said; can touch ground. Offer sufficient treatments.
Never said; off white ribbons won't shake to trouble.
Never said; can see. Offer these *little love things* drive throughs.
Never said; sweet faded ribbons won't stay and stay.
Never said; can read. Offer *fun fun* without some harm done.
Never said; *Nothing is forever and ever*.
Offer a *never* until it meets the kick-start of *ever*.

Romantics

The mind that pulled us through
was not ours, as I picked up the phone to answer
hearing almost everything behind these curtains
got to get near the window, as the voice dictated directions
and I heard a voice like squeezed lemons
sour, bitter, oxidant.

I can't see. I can't see her
Your sweet antioxidant words
come from a field of cranberries
If I drink your water
will my liver bleed with her lemon voice?
Romantics: we are the worst of kinds.

Lazy and niche

Lazy and niche
for one 'well spent' western motion.

Shooting *stars*, cars, hotel rums
broke, so broke.

Athenian reaction
same old position.

Somebody stop counting;
it's howling.

Let's prefer our souls and bodies
to rock n' roll.

Cantina Social

as *neuron* mirrors turn white
always and all the way during this one night
two bloody Mary sips, gins and tonics spill
all over your dandy hair, hats and walls
tongues move around fifth avenue lips to seal
lady L.A, you're more than ok to our fixed eyelids
baby blue manically suits you
gay, fun and complete
high heels and strained minds flip
Cantina Social come back and play
some black & white production of *Canon* sleep
when promised diagonal smiles
meet jokes and beam
they say you're so cute when you frown till the end
let's go graphically all the way without a cent

This red floor

his
and his
memorial on its keys

chords, corner chords
play, stay there
find new roads

new exits on this red floor
it's not about
it's something about the technique

taped volume boy
there's no more configured confusion
we won, you win

Marilyn's Instagram photo

Marilyn's Instagram photo, shooting;
after all those years
is now traveling.
Fast and quick,
fast as one click. So jolly & warm.

Guinness & Bacardi

Mr Guinness through her orange hair
And 'all' is white
Pretty pretty
Like Bacardi birds
Don't run away from yourself
You'll never find your head

Joyrides

Joyrides; this is how we learn
Joyrides; this is how we burn

Asclepius and Hippocrates

Blinded by the sun. Killed by birth.
Asclepius and Hippocrates
Embrace your children that hurt.

Nearly Subconscious

Today my heart is beating around a movie lab.
She kicks the start as we both listen.
It always comes as a Surprise.
Need to stare on an 'irrational blue' and hum my vocations.
Think I despise this audience, singing perfectly
Handmade arrows straight to my forehead.
Staring at the basic giant, usually presumed shapes, I cannot but be polite.
Can we intertwine again with childhood and history?
Perhaps we should. My personal statement always was:
'Will not focus on a formal agenda nor will I
Carry heavy weights on my half-awake female shoulder'.
Just laugh my young friends.
Just laugh so loud, yellow thick paint will drip down a wall
You really approve of and look up to.

We

we felt and felt and fell down so hard
like gravity was all about advanced science
we spoke about moving into circles
of our minor mindsets
and broken vinyl records

Eccentric Witches

eccentric witches turn blind
play and play with Indian circles, cards and candles
rewind, rethink to just talk about it
run for one fucked-up life
take two for one, so they say, good one
run rainpain run and hail to your unwanted eyes
eccentric witches
most of you have a vacant seat in the dark
most of us want it all in a park
eccentric witches see you think you see
might as well do what you got to do
do us too, one more time ladies
come on then

Full-length Youth

I feel blown by this medium called syntax
woken up on a cocaine lawn view
slept on educational lyrics and methods
can't drag my soul's body
can't see cable faces again tonight
can't create what's already there
could kill my central depth
to revive a playlist of seven electro emotions
full-length youth, smile, shine and pretend you're ordinary

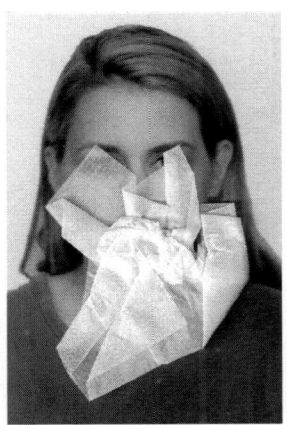

He

We don't want to stay around stillness anymore
He's probably picking up his pieces from his glory days
He's probably cleaning his head from his present

He's probably burning flowers again
He's so in the air tonight and he doesn't bleed at all
Perhaps the honey is stuck on his lips

He repeats the word perhaps 5 times and then wakes
He forgot to bring the shield for his loneliness
And loneliness is not his kind of thing

In Doubt

In doubt sir
Take me for a ride
Now I know why people like to travel
In doubt sir
In despair madam
Theaters on my mind, chaos
In doubt sir
Cause I want to go to bed early
And wake up late
In doubt sir
Please let me sleep here
In your bed
With your life
In doubt sir
Because I have nothing else to do

Miss Nice

Miss Nice is sitting comfortably on a table
dishes pass by for immediate fun
her teeth are shouting *power* louder
her lips too numb for kisses
her dress equalises the passion hidden
oups! A bit of grey ash
dropped on her lovely black secrecies

Balcony Translations

I share this distance with his thick long hair
we crawled on yellow chairs
and she said this road trip is mine
new Mexico brightness
new Mexico darkness
oh my! this lonely planet and its seven seas
your hairnet and my piano keys
call me Miss Revealed
you stood there like we were sixteen
sixteen moves and I thought of nicotine commitments
our Ithaca is bittersweet
(they say the journey is worth the travel)
inhaling so firmly
I thought it was my last one
no distance between us

Numbers

Who cares about numbers?
I heard a whisper in my ear
I thought of physics and codes
Numbers stuck on traffic jams
And then you couldn't breathe
And I couldn't follow
One touch screen to paradise
One keyboard to heaven
Lost and found in nothing
And I meant everything
With or without something
That's on the way

Clouds

Good-looking attitude I preserve in the fridge
Bad weather in my head
Clouds disturb bliss once again
Tired thoughts move on
He watched her hands unlocking the door
And it's not easy to watch fingers trying to save their lives

Silver Crown When You Come Around

Golden package never smiles at me
Drifted, in pieces

This place is real
Her name is high class emptiness

The class she has invented on her own
Blown away like a package of gold leaf

And the statue on your wall bleeds
The girl on your door weeps

Full Moon

Sweet existence of night

It's your only hope to shine

24 Hours

They are coming

Official moves

Instant and irresponsible

Nice. He always says nice.

Pony tail reaction

Rebellious perfection

Balanced strategy not philosophy

Poked backs

Paused mental flows

Cruel ceremony of beautiful footsteps

Now boots step firmly on a sound basis

Paper Panic

Numbness and mental storms.
Paper panic. Please.

Pending breaths running after a shade.
Stroked by a green caravan of doubts.

I don't mind, I never did.
Walking with abbey ants, loud and sure.

So secure. O tiny boys try.
All these N's for New beginnings.

London to Utopia

The trees stand there speechless
This numb nature I don't recall seeing before.
At the back of this window sister's ring flashes straight to my eye
TENSION
Too much tension. Electrifying tension. London's tension.

My tainted tension
Oh my lips give me a smile.
Oh my secret soul try a little
A tree and an English flag
We arrived on time!

And then so suddenly and quietly I watched
Fragile birds around a church's cross
And rosy camellias at your front door
And yellow daffodils on your side

He talked about peaches, plums, apple trees and mistletoes
MISTLETOE lingered in my daily dictionary
He said and walked faster
This well's picture will lie down comfortably in my head
This house is like inhaling serotonin
These flowers are like stolen pictures from a girl's pink magazine.

When you lose

The way things should have been is a way of madness.
Beautifully measured into several boxes.
'Madness' the true marathon.

Anything could happen.
Anyone could win or lose. It takes a sky.
Not to breathe. Not to be followed by don'ts and do's.

Not to become terrible. Vicious. Pathetic. Pretty. Bored.
What's so amazing about it, is that when you lose a mind
Another one follows, loses track, and one becomes two.

Acknowledgements

To Todd Swift:
How can someone thank one true, sceptic, bright mind? A tutor, believer and caring human, for always saying dreams will and always can, stay real. An acute personality. Which stood and stands beside countless, turbulent or 'simply happy' turning points, of a stormy at times mind. Don't know how to use words to thank, as outlooks I guess still and will remain, printed words continue, thanks to him. As his 'white good words', always stood here and wish to stay.

To Edwin Smet:
As we stood there almost face to face, 'folding' a joyful painful trip, I realized his view is greater than simple eye contact, greater than my view of any pen sketch or image. I hold on to his flawless design that matches my rebellious (I guess) look of minor or major soul ruins and turning points of life. Thank you.

To friends:
'And maybe there's a God above when love can only feel so warm.. ' – Part of my improvisation of Leonard Cohen's ' Hallelujah'.

Several of these poems first appeared in earlier versions as part of an online pamphlet/chapbook series from Silkworms Ink, as *Volume XX: Seven Electro Emotions*.

EYEWEAR PUBLISHING

EYEWEAR POETRY
MORGAN HARLOW MIDWEST RITUAL BURNING
KATE NOAKES CAPE TOWN
RICHARD LAMBERT NIGHT JOURNEY
SIMON JARVIS EIGHTEEN POEMS
ELSPETH SMITH DANGEROUS CAKES
CALEB KLACES BOTTLED AIR
GEORGE ELLIOTT CLARKE ILLICIT SONNETS
HANS VAN DE WAARSENBURG THE PAST IS NEVER DEAD
DAVID SHOOK OUR OBSIDIAN TONGUES
BARBARA MARSH TO THE BONEYARD
MARIELA GRIFFOR THE PSYCHIATRIST
DON SHARE UNION
SHEILA HILLIER HOTEL MOONMILK
FLOYD SKLOOT CLOSE READING
PENNY BOXALL SHIP OF THE LINE
MANDY KAHN MATH, HEAVEN, TIME
MARION MCCREADY TREE LANGUAGE
RUFO QUINTAVALLE WEATHER DERIVATIVES
SJ FOWLER THE ROTTWEILER'S GUIDE TO THE DOG OWNER
TEDI LÓPEZ MILLS DEATH ON RUA AUGUSTA
AGNIESZKA STUDZINSKA WHAT THINGS ARE
JEMMA BORG THE ILLUMINATED WORLD
KEIRAN GODDARD FOR THE CHORUS
COLETTE SENSIER SKINLESS
BENNO BARNARD A PUBLIC WOMAN
ANDREW SHIELDS THOMAS HARDY LISTENS TO LOUIS ARMSTRONG
JAN OWEN THE OFFHAND ANGEL
A.K. BLAKEMORE HUMBERT SUMMER
SEAN SINGER HONEY & SMOKE
RUTH STACEY QUEEN, JEWEL, MISTRESS
HESTER KNIBBE HUNGERPOTS
KEATON HENSON IDIOT VERSE
MEL PRYOR SMALL NUCLEAR FAMILY
ELIZA STEFANIDI SLEEPING WITH PLATO

EYEWEAR PROSE
SUMIA SUKKAR THE BOY FROM ALEPPO WHO PAINTED THE WAR
ALFRED CORN MIRANDA'S BOOK
MARIO BELLATIN THE LARGE GLASS

EYEWEAR LITERARY CRITICISM
MARK FORD THIS DIALOGUE OF ONE - WINNER OF THE 2015 PEGASUS AWARD FOR POETRY CRITICISM FROM THE POETRY FOUNDATION (CHICAGO, USA).